Washington D.C.

W9-BJA-413

I.S.B.N. 1-879295-08-3
Published by **L.B. Prince Co., Inc.**
6621-C Electronic Drive
Springfield, VA 22151
Designed and Published in USA
Printed in Italy by **Kina Italia**

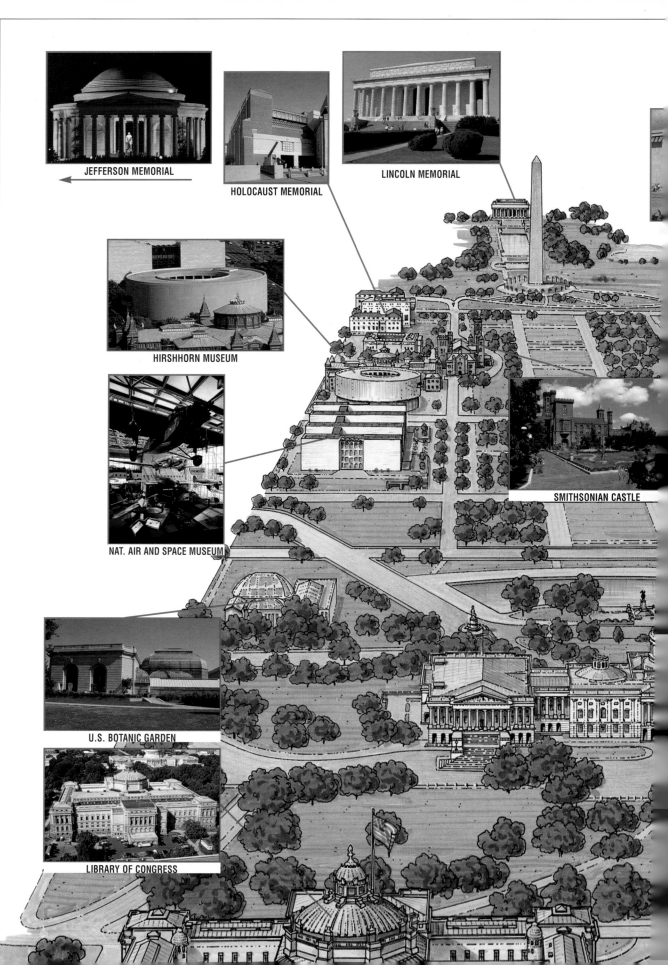

JEFFERSON MEMORIAL

HOLOCAUST MEMORIAL

LINCOLN MEMORIAL

HIRSHHORN MUSEUM

NAT. AIR AND SPACE MUSEUM

SMITHSONIAN CASTLE

U.S. BOTANIC GARDEN

LIBRARY OF CONGRESS

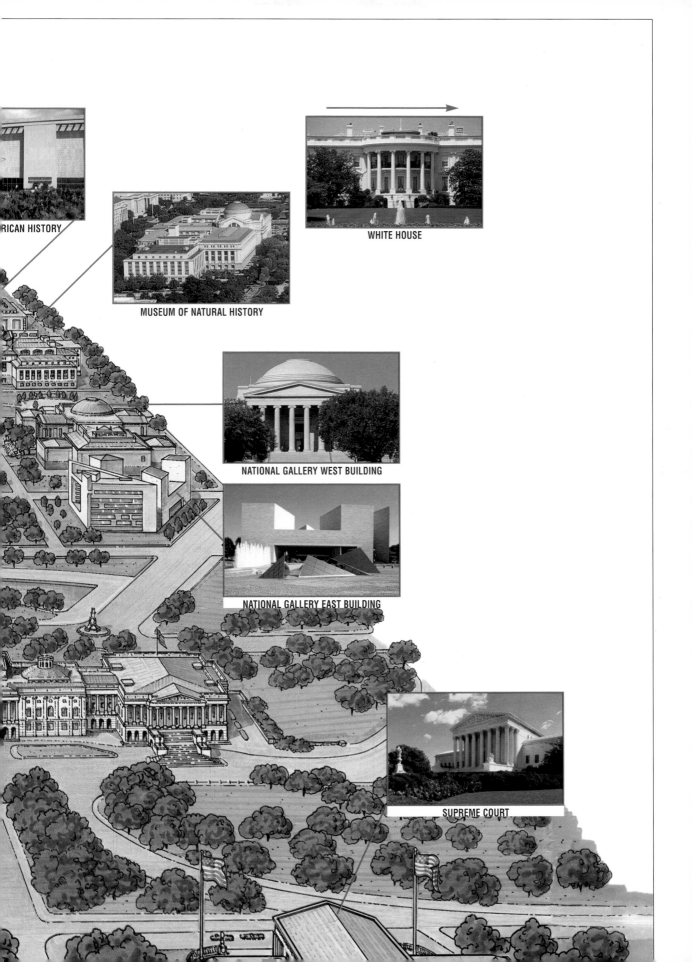

RICAN HISTORY

MUSEUM OF NATURAL HISTORY

WHITE HOUSE

NATIONAL GALLERY WEST BUILDING

NATIONAL GALLERY EAST BUILDING

SUPREME COURT

WASHINGTON, D.C.

In less than 200 years one of the world's most beautiful cities has emerged from what was virtually nothing more than a marshy wilderness. Containing the central governmental seat of a prosperous and powerful nation, Washington, D.C. has been the Capital of the United States since 1800. The plans for it were begun in 1791 when the first President of the United States, George Washington, selected this site, and then chose Pierre Charles L'Enfant as the man to design the city. Paris-born L'Enfant was an engineer in the Continental Army and his sweeping design for the Capital City was patterned in part on the splendid expanses of Versailles.

The efforts of Thomas Jefferson and Alexander Hamilton were extremely instrumental during the controversy of a proposed site for the Capital. Many previous attempts to select a place failed owing to the political rivalry between the states, and between 1783 and 1790, Congress considered various sites for the new Nation's capital, but was unable to reach an agreement. At one time it authorized work on a site near Trenton, New Jersey; later chose Germantown, Pennsylvania, and in the meantime, settled down in Philadelphia, Pennsylvania as a temporary capital. By 1790, feelings were so strong over the issue of where the Capital was to be located, that the South threatened to break away from the Union. Wisely, Jefferson and Hamilton reached a compromise: Jefferson would endorse Hamilton's proposal for Federal Government assumption of State war debts, if Hamilton would endorse a site on the Potomac for the new capital. Both bills passed, and President Washington was able to make his selection. He decided upon a site of 10 square miles lying on both sides of the Potomac River. The northern part was ceded by Maryland and the southern by Virginia. Later the southern portion was returned to Virginia and the "Territory of Columbia" (as it was known at the time) became the city of "Washington". Pierre Charles l'Enfant planned and designed the city with great foresight. L'Enfant selected Capitol Hill as the focal point and laid out broad avenues which radiate like the spokes of a wheel from centers placed within the rectangular pattern of the streets. Although L'Enfant's handsome plan was in the end changed a great deal, his wide avenues and sweeping vistas combined with monumental buildings make the Capital unique among American Cities.

On August 24, 1814, during the War of 1812, the British took the city and over the next few days burned all the public buildings except the combined post and patent offices. The White House was rebuilt by 1817 and two years later the Capitol Building again was ready for use.

In its early days, the city centered around Lafayette Square, reaching east to the Capitol and west to old Georgetown. Many of the colonial houses are still standing in these areas, and many more well worth seeing can be found in nearby Virginia. Now the capital reflects various styles of architectural design although most of it conforms to the classical Greek and Roman. Its imposing buildings are seldom over four or five stories in height and hundreds of monuments and memorials honor the heroes and statesmen of America and its allies. Noted for its art galleries and museums, there are now legitimate theaters, and a fine symphony orchestra. With few exceptions, most of the great landmarks are only a short distance apart.

The city's population has grown rapidly. In 1840 it was 44,000 and by 1860 the population had reached 75,000. Today, Washington has a population of over 750,000 about two-thirds of which work for the Federal Government.

In 1900, Washington celebrated the 100th Anniversary of the removal of the seat of Government to the District of Columbia. The population then was 278,218. Cable cars were being replaced by electric cars and horse drawn vehicles were giving way to automobiles. Railroad tracks still lay on the Mall and the sites of the Lincoln and Jefferson Memorials were a swamp land. William McKinley was President and Theodore Roosevelt was Vice-President. The District at that time had a veterinarian on its payroll as there were 500 horses and mules in service.

As L'Enfant planned, Washington has vast acreages of parks, squares, circles and open space. While it is important as the center of the U.S. Federal Government, it is also a great cultural center containing numerous museums, art galleries, libraries, shrines, churches, parks and monumental buildings. It is no wonder that each year, millions of visitors from all parts of the world come to see this magnificent city, less than 200 years old, but already so richly endowed with beauty and American history.

WASHINGTON, D.C.

...une des plus belles villes-capitales du monde; ...e a été créée en moins de 200 ans sur une ...rre marécageuse et inculte. Siège central ...ouvernamental d'une nation florissante et ...issante, Washington, D.C. est la Capitale du ...ouvernement des Etats-Unis depuis 1800. Les ...ans de la ville remontent à 1791, date à laquelle ...premier Président des Etats-Unis, George ...ashington, choisit cet emplacement et chargea ...erre Charles L'Enfant de tracer les plans de la ...le. Né à Paris, L'Enfant était ingénieur dans ...rmée Continentale; il s'inspira, en partie, pour ...n projet d'ensemble, des splendides étendues ...e Versailles.

...s efforts de Thomas Jefferson et d'Alexandre ...amilton furent extrêmement pragmatiques au ...urs de la polémique qui enfiévra les esprits au ...jet du choix de l'emplacement de la capitale. ...usieurs tentatives précédentes échouèrent à ...use de la rivalité politique qui divisait les états ...entre 1783 et 1790, le Congrès examina divers ...nplacements sur lesquels la capitale de la jeune ...tion aurait pu être bâtie sans toutefois arriver à ...accord. A un moment donné, le Congrès ...nna son accord pour entreprendre les travaux ...ns une région située à proximité de Trenton, ...ns le New Jersey, puis il porta son choix sur ...ermantown, en Pennsylvanie, et s'installa, ...tre-temps, à Philadelphie, Pennsylvanie, qui ...vint la capitale provisoire. En 1790, les esprits ...aient tellement échauffés au sujet de la décision ...i devait être prise quant à l'emplacement de la ...pitale, que le Sud menaça la sécession. ...gement, Jefferson et Hamilton arrivèrent à un ...mpromis: Jefferson acceptait la proposition de ...amilton qui demandait que le Gouvernement ...déral prenne à sa charge les dettes de la ...erre de l'Etat, à condition que Hamilton appuie ...choix d'un emplacement de la nouvelle capitale ...r le Potomac. Les deux décrets passèrent au ...ongrès, furent votés et le Président Washington ...t enfin faire son choix. Il opta pour une terre de ...miles mètres carrés qui s'étendait des deux ...tés du fleuve Potomac. La partie nord était ...dée par le Maryland et la partie sud par la ...rginie. Plus tard, la portion sud restituée à la ...rginie et le "Territoire de Columbia" (comme on ...ppelait à l'époque) devint la ville de Washington. ...erre Charles l'Enfant étudia le projet et traça les ...ans de la ville avec une claire vision de l'avenir. ...hoisit Capitol Hill comme point central et il ...ssina de larges avenues qui partaient en étoile ...mme les rayons d'une roue de centres placés à ...térieur du quadrilatère qui formait les rues. ...algré d'importantes modifications qui furent ...portées par la suite à son plan, ses larges ...enues et ses profondes échappées et ses ...nstructions monumentales font de cette capitale ...e ville unique en Amérique.

...24 août 1814, pendant la guerre de 1812, les ...glais prirent la ville et brûlèrent au cours des ...urs qui suivirent tous les édifices publics à ...xception du bâtiment qui abritait les bureaux de ...poste et des brevets. La Maison-Blanche fut

reconstruite en 1817 et, deux ans plus tard, le Capitole était de nouveau terminé et disponible. Au début, la ville était concentrée autour du Square Lafayette et atteignait, à l'est le Capitole et, à l'ouest, la vieille Georgetown. Bon nombre de maisons coloniales sont encore debout dans ces quartiers et d'autres, bien plus nombreuses et intéressantes à visiter, peuvent être découvertes et admirées pour leur architecture variée, avec une certaine prépondérance du style Grec et Romain classique. Ses édifices, imposants, dépassent rarement quatre ou cinq étages et des centaines de monuments commémoratifs honorent les héros et les hommes d'Etat de l'Amérique et de ses alliés. Outre ses galeries d'art et ses musées, elle offre aujourd'hui des salles de spectacles renommées et un excellent orchestre symphonique. A part quelques rares exceptions, la plupart des centres d'intérêt sont concentrés dans des zones rapprochées.

La population de la ville s'est rapidement accrue. En 1840 elle était de 44.000 habitants, en 1860 elle s'élevait à 75.000. Aujourd'hui, Washington compte plus de 750.000 habitants dont les deux tiers environ travaillent pour le Gouvernement Fédéral. En 1900, Washington célébra le centième anniversaire du transfert du Siège du Gouvernement dans le District de Columbia. La population s'élevait à cette époque à 278.718 habitants. Les trams traînés par câble furent remplacés par les trams électriques et les véhicules traînés par des chevaux firent place aux automobiles. Les rails dans le Mall existent encore et les monuments commémoratifs à Lincoln et Jefferson se dressaient, alors, sur un terrain marécageux.

William McKinley était Président et Théodore Roosevelt Vice-Président. Le District avait, à cette époque, un vétérinaire public car 500 chevaux et mulets étaient de service. Conformément au plan de l'Enfant, Washington possède de vastes parcs, squares, places et espaces verts. Siège du Gouvernement Fédéral des Etats-Unis, Washington est aussi un grand centre culturel grâce à ses nombreux musées, galeries d'art, bibliothèques, chapelles, églises, parcs et constructions monumentales. Il n'est pas étonnant que des millions de touristes affluent des quatre coins du monde pour visiter, tous les ans, cette ville magnifique, qui n'est pas encore bicentaire mais déjà si pleine de charme et imprégnée d'histoire américaine.

WASHINGTON, D.C.

In weniger als 200 Jahren enstand hier eine der schönsten Städte der Welt, wo davor praktisch nichts anderes als unwegsame Wildnis herrschte. Als zentraler Regierungssitz einer blühenden und mächtigen Nation ist Washington seit dem Jahre 1800 die Hauptstadt der Regierung der Vereinigten Staaten.

Die Pläne zu der Stadtgründung gehen zurück auf das Jahr 1791, als George Washington, der erste Präsident der Vereinigten Staaten, den Ort auswählte; danach beauftragte er Pierre Charles L'Enfant mit der Planung der Stadt. Der in Paris gebürtige L'Enfant war Ingenieur in der Europäischen Armee, und sein überwältigender Entwurf für diese Hauptstadt war stark geprägt von den weitläufigen Ausmaßen von Versailles.

Die Zusammenarbeit von Thomas Jefferson und Alexander Hamilton war äußerst zweckmäßig, zumal hinsichtlich der Wahl des Ortes für die zu errichtende Hauptstadt große Meinungsverschiedenheiten bestanden. Alle früheren Versuche, einen geeigneten Platz auszuwählen, scheiterten an der Rivalitätspolitik der einzelnen Staaten; in den Jahren zwischen 1783 und 1790 schlug der Kongreß etliche Plätze für die neue Hauptstadt vor, aber es konnte keine Einigung erzielt werden. Einmal hatte man sich fast bereits für ein Gebiet in der Nähe von Trenton in New Jersey entschlossen, ein andermal dachte man an Germantown in Pennsylvania - während sich in der Zwischenzeit notgedrungenerweise eine Art Haupstadt in Philadelphia, Pennsylvania, vorläufig bildete. Im Jahre 1790, als man immer noch zu keiner Einigung gelangt war, wo nun denn die neue Hauptstadt anzusiedeln sei, drohte der Süden mit seiner Loslösung von der Union. Klugerweise gelangten dann Jefferson und Hamilton zu einer Einigung: Jefferson akzeptierte Hamiltons Vorschlag, die Staatskriegsschulden durch die Bundersregierung tilgen zu lassen, vorausgesetzt, daß Hamilton der Gründung der neuen Hauptstadt am Potomac-Fluß zustimmen würde. Beide Vorschläge wurden angenommen, so daß Präsident Washington nun seinen Vorschlag zur Ortswahl durchsetzen konnte.

Er entschied sich für eine Fläche von über 10 Quadratmeilen beiderseits des Potomac-Flusses. An dieses Areal grenzte im Norden Maryland und im Süden Virginia. Später wurde der südliche Teil an Virginia zurückerstattet, und das "Territorial von Columbia" - als solches war es damals bekannt - wurde nun die Stadt Washington.

Pierre Charles L'Enfant hatte die Stadt in weiser Voraussicht geplant und entworfen. L'Enfant hatte den Kapitol-Hügel als Brennpunkt auserwählt, von dem aus breite Alleen wie Speichen eines Rades gehen, die sich harmonisch dem rasterartigen Straßensystem einordnen lassen. Obwohl L'Enfants Entwurf letztlich groben Veränderungen unterworfen wurde, bildete die Hauptstadt mit ihren großzügigen Prachtstraßen und Denkmälern eine Einheit, einzigartige Ausnahme unter den amerikanischen Städten.

Am 24. August 1814, mitten im Krieg von 1812, eroberten die Engländer die Stadt und brannten innerhalb weniger Tage sämtliche öffentlichen Gebäude mit Ausnahme des Bürobaues der Post und des Patentamtes nieder. Das Weiße Haus wurde im Jahre 1817 wieder aufgebaut, und zwei Jahre später konnte auch das Kapitol wieder bezogen werden.

In der ersten Bestehenszeit bildet der Lafayette-Platz das Stadtzentrum, das sich im Osten bis zum Kapitol und im Westen zum alten Georgetown erstreckte. Noch heute befinden sich in dieser Gegend viele Häuser im Kolonialstil, und noch viele mehr und wirklich sehenswerte kann man noch in Virginia finden. Heute spiegelt die Hauptstadt viele architektonische Stile wieder, aber die meisten halten sich an die griechische und römische Klassik. Ihre Kolossalbauten ragen nur selten über die Höhe von vier oder fünf Stockwerken empor; Hunderte von Monumenten und Gedächtnisstätten ehrten die Helden und Staatsmänner von Amerika und seinen Verbündeten. Es ist bekannt für seine Kunstgalerien und Museen und verfügt heute über selbstständige Theatergruppen und ein ausgezeichnetes Symphonieorchester. Mit nur ganz wenigen Ausnahmen sind sämtliche wichtigen Sehenswürdigkeiten nur unweit entfernt. Die Stadtbevölkerung ist rapid gewachsen. Während man im Jahr 1840 noch 44.000 Einwohner zählte, waren es um 1860 bereits 75.000 Einwohner, von denen ungefähr zwei Drittel für die Bundesregierung arbeiteten.

Im Jahre 1900 feierte Washington den hundertsten Jahrestag der Zugestehung des Regierungssitzes im Bezirk von Columbia. Damals zählte die Bevölkerung ca. 278.718. Cablecars wurden durch elektrische Tramways ersetzt, und die privaten Pferdegespanne und Kutschen mußten dem Automobil weichen. Noch heute kann man die Straßenbahnschienen am Mall und in der Nähe der Denkmäler Lincolns und Jeffersons entdecken. Dahinter herrschte damals freies Land. William McKinley war damals Präsident, und Theodore Roosevelt erfüllte seine Pflicht als Vizepräsident. Die Gemeinde mußte damals einen Tierarzt erhalten, und es gab über 500 Pferde und Maultiere im Dienst.

Der Planung L'Enfants getreu verfügt Washington auch heute noch über riesige Parkflächen, Plätze, baumbestandene Rundflächen und Grünanlagen. Es ist nicht nur als Regierungssitz der Bundesregierung der Vereinigten Staaten von immenser Bedeutung, sondern auch als kulturelles Zentrum mit seinen zahlreichen Museen und Kunstgalerien, Bibliotheken, Mausoleen, Kirchen, Parkanlagen und Monumentalbauten. So ist es kein Wunder, daß jedes Jahr Millionen von Besuchern von allen Teilen der Welt angereist kommen, um diese herrliche Stadt kennenzulernen, die trotz ihres jungen Bestehens von weniger als 200 Jahren bereits so reich mit Schönheit und amerikanischer Geschichte gesegnet ist.

WASHINGTON, D.C.

En menos de 200 años, una de las ciudades capitales más bellas del mundo ha emergido de lo que no era virtualmente más que un desierto pantanoso.

Conteniendo la sede central del gobierno de una nación prospera, Washington, D.C. ha sido la capital del gobierno de los Estados Unidos desde 1800. Los planes para ello fueron comenzados en 1791 cuando el primer Presidente de los Estados Unidos, George Washington, escogió este lugar, y luego designó a Pierre Charles L'Enfant como al hombre que habría de diseñar la ciudad.

L'Enfant, nacido en Paris, era un ingeniero en el ejercito Continental y su diseño en esquema para la Ciudad Capital estaba inspirado en parte en los espléndidos espacios de Versalles.

Los esfuerzos de Thomas Jefferson y de Alexander Hamilton fueron extremadamente instrumentales durante la controversia acerca del lugar propuesto para la capital. Muchos intentos precedentes de seleccionar un sitio habían fracasado a causa de las rivalidades políticas entre los estados y entre 1738 y 1790, el Congreso consideró varios lugares para situar en ellos a la capital de la Nación, pero no fu capaz de llegar a un acuerdo. Una vez se autorizó el comienzo de los trabajos en un lugar cerca de Trenton, New Jersey; más tarde se escogió Germantown, Pennsylvania, y mientras tanto, se instaló en Filadelfia, Pennsylvania, como en una capital provisional. Hacia 1790, los ánimos estaban tan excitados respecto al éxito de la cuestión de donde se iba a localizar por fin a la capital, que el Sur amenazó una secesión por este motivo. Muy astutamente, Jefferson y Hamilton llegaron a un compromiso: Jefferson habría apoyado la propuesta de Hamilton para que el gobierno Federal aceptase las deudas de guerra del Estado, si Hamilton apoyaba la elección de un lugar en el Potomac para la nueva capital. Los dos proyectos de ley fueron aprobados y el Presidente Washington pudo hacer su selección. Se decidió por un lugar de 10 millas cuadradas situado a ambas partes del Río Potomac. La parte norte fu cedida por Maryland y la parte sur por Virginia. Más tarde, la parte sur se devolvió a Virginia y el "Territorio de Columbia" (como era conocido en aquella época), se convirtió en la ciudad de "Washington".

Pierre Charles L'Enfant hizo los planes y diseñó la ciudad con gran precisión. L'Enfant escogió la Colina del Capitolio como el punto focal y dispuso amplias avenidas que irradiaban como los radios de una rueda desde centros situados dentro del perímetro rectangular de las calles. Aunque el hermoso plano de l'Enfant fue bastante cambiado al final, sus amplias avenidas y sus panoramas extensos combinados con edificios monumentales hicieron de la Capital una ciudad única entre la Ciudades Americanas.

El 24 de Agosto de 1814, durante la guerra del 1812, los ingleses tomaron la ciudad y durante los días siguientes quemaron todas las oficinas públicas excepto las oficinas combinadas de correo y patentes. La Casa Blanca fu reconstruida hacia 1817 y dos años más tarde el Edificio del Capitolio estaba de nuevo listo para ser utilizado. En sus primeros dias, el centro de la ciudad se extendía alrededor de la Plaza de Lafayette, alcanzando al Este el Capitolio y al Oeste la vieja Georgetown. Muchas de la s casas coloniales todavía están en pie en estas zonas y muchas otras, que valen más la pena de ser vistas, pueden encontrarse en las cercanías de Virginia. Actualmente la Capital refleja varios estilos de diseño arquitectónico, aunque la mayor parte de la misma se inspira en el diseño clásico Griego y Romano. Sus edificios imponentes tienen raramente más de cuatro o cinco pisos de altura y centenares de monumentos y lugares conmemorativos honran a los héroes y a los hombres de Estado de América y de sus aliados. Ya conocida por sus galerías de arte y sus museos, ahora tiene también teatros válidos y una orquestra sinfónica excelente. Con pocas excepciones, la mayor parte de los lugares importantes se encuentran a poca distancia entre ellós.

La población de la ciudad creció rápidamente. En 1840 era de 44.000 personas y hacia 1860 la población había alcanzado la cifra de 75.000 habitantes.

Hoy en día, Washington tiene una población de más de 750.000 personas, alrededor de dos tercios de las cuales trabajan para el Gobierno Federal.

En 1900, Washington celebró el Centenario del desplazamiento de la sede del Gobierno al Distrito de Columbia. La población entonces era de 278.218 habitantes. Los tranvías movidos por tracción de cable estaban siendo sustituidos por tranvías eléctricos, y los vehículos movidos por caballos empezaban a dejar el paso a los automóviles. Huellas de carriles quedan en el Mall y los sitios que ahora ocupan los monumentos conmemorativos de Lincoln y de Jefferson eran un tiempo un terreno pantanoso. William McKinley era el Presidente y Theodore Roosevelt era el vicepresidente. El distrito en aquella época tenía a un veterinario en su nómina de sueldos ya que había entonces 500 caballos y mulos en servicio. Como l'Enfant había planeado, Washington tiene muchos acres de parques, plazas, glorietas y espacio abierto. Así como es importante por ser el centro del gobierno Federal de los Estados Unidos, es también un gran centro cultural que contiene numerosos museos, galerías de arte, bibliotecas, capillas, iglesias, parques y edificios monumentales.

No sorprende que cada año, millones de visitantes de todas partes del mundo vengan a visitar ésta magnifica ciudad, de menos de 200 años de antigedad, pero ya tan ricamente dotada de belleza y de historia Americana.

ワシントン D.C.

　今から２００年近く前、事実上何もない未開の湿地帯にすぎなかったところに、この世界でもっとも美しい都市の一つが誕生した。豊かな大国の中央政府の所在地ワシントンD.C.は、１８００年からアメリカ合衆国の首都となっている。１７９１年に初代大統領ジョージ・ワシントンがこの場所を選び、都市設計者としてピエール・シャルル・ランファンを任命したときからこの計画は始まった。パリ生まれのランファンは植民地軍の技師であり、首都の全体的デザインは広々とした美しいヴェルサイユに一部基づいている。

　トーマス・ジェファーソンとアレキサンダー・ハミルトンの努力が首都の候補地を巡る論争の解決に大きな力を果たした。それまでにも首都を決定しようとする多くの試みがあったが、州間の政治的対立によってすべて失敗に終わっていた。１７８３年から１７９０年にかけて、議会は新しい首都のさまざまな候補地を検討したが、いずれも合意には至らなかった。一時ニュージャージー州のトレントン近くの用地への建設が認められ、その後ペンシルベニア州ジャーマンタウンが選ばれている。その間、ペンシルバニアのフィラデルフィアが臨時首都に定められた。１７９０年には首都をどこにするかという議論に対する反感から、南部が連合を離脱する恐れが生じていた。ここでジェファーソンとハミルトンは賢明にも妥協に達したのである。それは、もしハミルトンが新しい首都としてポトマック河畔を認めるならば、独立戦争で各州が被った負債を連邦政府が補填するというハミルトンの提案をジェファーソンが支持するというものだった。両法案は議会を通過し、ワシントン大統領は自らの選択を行うことができた。彼はポトマック川の両岸にまたがる１０平方マイルの土地に首都を建設することにし、北岸はメリーランド州、南岸はヴァージニア州から譲渡を受けた。後に南の部分はヴァージニア州に返還され、〈コロンビア地域〉（当時の呼び名）は〈ワシントン〉市となった。ピエール・シャルル・ランファンは都市の設計とデザインを非常な先見の明をもって行った。ランファンは国会議事堂の丘を焦点として選び、道路の作る長方形のパターンの中を、車のスポークのように中心から放射状に伸びる広いアヴェニューを設計した。ランファンのみごとなプランは最終的には大きく変更されたが、広々としたアヴェニューと見通しのいい眺望が堂々たる建物と結び付き、首都ワシントンは合衆国の中でユニークな都市となっている。

　１８１２年の戦争の際、１８１４年８月２４日にはイギリス軍が町を占領し、郵便局と特許局の入った建物を除き、公共建築物をその後数日のうちにすべて焼き払った。ホワイトハウスは１８１７年に再建され、その２年後には国会議事堂が再び利用できるようになった。

　建設当初、市の中心はラファイエット広場周辺にあり、東は国会議事堂、西は旧ジョージタウンに達していた。今もこの辺りにはコロニアル風の家が多く見られるが、隣のヴァージニア州にはさらに多くの一見に値する家が残っている。現在、ワシントンにはさまざまな様式の建築があるが、中でもっとも多いのは古典的なギリシアとローマの様式である。

　市の堂々とした建物はほとんど４、５階を越えることはなく、市内にはまたアメリカとその同盟国の英雄や政治家の名誉を称える何百という記念碑や記念館がある。美術館や博物館は以前から有名だったが、現在では本格的な劇場とすばらしい交響楽団もよく知られるようになった。少しの例外を除いて、主要な文化財の大部分はわずかな距離の範囲に集中している。

　市の人口は急速に増加し、１８４０年の４万４千人から１８６０年には７万５千人に達した。今日ではワシントンの人口は７５万人以上を数え、そのおよそ３分の２が連邦政府の職員である。ワシントンでは１９００年にコロンビア特別区への遷都百周年の祝典が催された。当時の人口は２７万８２１８人と記録されている。ケーブルカーに代わって電車、馬車に代わって自動車が走り始めた時期である。モール地区を鉄道が走り、リンカーンとジェファーソンの記念碑の建てられた場所は沼沢地であった。ウィリアム・マッキンリーが大統領で、セオドア・ルーズヴェルトが副大統領だったころである。馬とロバ合わせて５００匹が使われていたから、当時の特別区の職員名簿には獣医の名も見える。

　ランファンの設計どおり、ワシントンには広大な面積の公園、広場、緑地がある。連邦政府の中心として重要であるだけでなく、ワシントンは偉大な文化の中心地でもあり、数多くの博物館、美術館、図書館、廟、教会、公園、記念建造物に囲まれている。毎年世界中から何百万人もの旅行者が、誕生してから２００年足らずでありながら、アメリカの歴史によって美しく彩られたこのすばらしい都市を訪れているのは当然といえるだろう。

The dome of the United States Capitol crowned with the Statue of Freedom.

La coupole du Capitole des Etats-Unis couronnée par la Statue de la Liberté.

Die Kuppel des Kapitols der Vereinigten Staaten gekrönt von der Freiheitsstatue.

La Cúpula del Capitolio de los Estados Unidos coronada por la Estatua de la Libertad.

頂に自由の像を載せたアメリカ合衆国国会議事堂のドーム。

President George Washington laid the cornerstone of the United States Capitol on September 18, 1793. The design for this impressive building resulted from a contest in which seventeen contestants submitted plans for the Capitol. The winner was an amateur designer, Dr. William Thornton. By 1827, the Capitol was completed according to his plans. Between 1851 and 1863, the Capitol was enlarged and a new dome was added. The east front was extended in 1958, but the original character of the building designed by Thornton has remained.

Le 18 septembre 1793, le Président George Washington posa la première pierre du Capitole des Etats-Unis. Le plan de cet impressionnant bâtiment fut choisi parmi dix-sept autres, autant de concurrents qui avaient présenté leurs projets. Le gagnant fut un dessinateur amateur, le Dr. William Thornton. En 1827, le Capitole était terminé conformément au plan original. Entre 1851 et 1863, il fut agrandi: un nouveau dôme lui fut ajouté et, en 1958, la façade fut agrandie; mais, malgré ces modifications, la construction a conservé son caractère d'origine tel qu'il avait été conçu par Thorton.

Präsident George Washington legte am 18. September 1793 den Grundstein des Kapitols der Vereinigten Staaten. Der Entwurf für dieses eindrucksvolle Gebäude war das Ergebnis eines Wettbewerbs, an dem siebzehn Teilnehmer ihre Ideen zur Ausstattung des Kapitols präsentierten. Gewinner war der Amateurdesigner Dr. William Thornton. Seinen Plänen getreu wurde das Kapitol im Jahre 1827 fertiggestellt. In den Jahren zwischen 1851 und 1863 wurde das Kapitol vergrößert und mit einer neuen Kuppel versehen. Im Jahre 1985 wurde die Ostseite èrweitert, aber der von Thornton geprägte ursprüngliche Charakter des Gebäudes blieb erhalten.

El presidente George Washington puso la primera piedra del Capitolio de los Estados Unidos el 18 de Septiembre de 1793. El diseño de éste impresionante edificio era el resultado de una competición en la que diecisiete participantes habían presentado planos para el Capitolio. El ganador fue un dibujante aficionado, Dr. William Thornton. En 1817, el Capitolio estaba ya terminado siguiendo sus planos. Entre 1851 y 1863, el Capitolio fue ampliado y se le añadió una nueva cúpula. La fachada de éste se amplió en 1958, pero se ha conservado el carácter original del edificio proyectado por Thornton.

１７９３年９月１８日に大統領
ジョージ・ワシントンによって合衆国
国会議事堂の定礎式が行われた。この
荘厳な建物のデザインを決定するための
コンクールには１７名が参加し、議事堂
の設計図を提出した。優勝者は
アマチュアのデザイナー、ウィリアム・
ソーントン博士で、１８２７年に彼の
設計どおりの議事堂が完成した。
１８５１年から１８６３年にかけて
議事堂は拡張され、新しいドームが
加えられた。東側は１９５８年に
広げられたが、ソーンソンが設計した
建物の本来の特徴は保たれている。

The Capitol is surrounded by a 68-acre park designed by Frederick Law Olmsted which includes many noble old trees, fountains and statues.

Le Capitole est entouré d'un parc qui s'étend sur 68 acres, dessiné par Frederick Law Olmsted; il abrite un grand nombre d'arbres centenaires, des fontaines et des statues.

Das Kapitol ist von einem Morgen (ca. 27 Hektar) großen Park umgeben, der nach Plänen von Frederick Law Olmsted angelegt wurde. In diesem Park wachsen viele majestätische, alte Bäume, und man findet viele Springbrunnen und Statuen.

El Capitolio está rodeado por un parque de 68 acres diseñado por Frederick Law Olmsted que contiene muchos viejos y nobles árboles, fuentes y estatuas.

議事堂を取り囲むフレデリック・ロー・オームステッド設計の68エーカーに及ぶ公園には、樹齢を重ねた大木、噴水、彫像などが数多くある。

One of three House Office Buildings which accommodate the offices of the members of the House of Representatives.
One of two Senate Office Buildings where Members of the Senate have their offices. Both the House and Senate Office Buildings are conveniently connected with the Capitol by an underground subway system.
The Folger Shakespeare Library contains the greatest collection of the early editions of Shakespeare in the world.

Un des trois bâtiments (House Office Building) où se trouvent les bureaux des membres de l'Assemblée Nationale. Un des deux bâtiments du Sénat où se trouvent les bureaux des Sénateurs. Les édifices, tant de l'Assemblée que du Sénat, communiquent avec le Capitole par un système de passages souterrains.
La ''Folger Shakespeare Library'' abrite la plus importante collection des éditions les plus récentes des oeuvres de Shakespeare publiées dans le monde entier.

Eines der drei Regierungsgebäude, die die einzelnen Büros der Abgeordneten beherbergen. Eines der beiden Senatsgebäude, wo die Senatsmitglieder ihre Büros haben. Sowohl die Regierungs- wie auch die Senatsbüros sind mit dem Kapitol durch ein bequemes Untergrundbahnsystem verbunden.
Die Folger Shakespeare Bücherei enthält die umfassendste Sammlung früher Shakespeare Ausgaben der Welt.

Uno de los tres Edificios que contienen las oficinas de los miembros de la Cámara de Representantes.
Uno de los dos Edificios del Senado donde los Miembros del Senado tienen sus oficinas. Tanto la Cámara como los Edificios enlazados del Senado están oportunamente conectados con el Capitolio por medio de un sistema de pasajes subterráneos.
La Biblioteca Folger Shakespeare contiene la más grande colección del mundo de las primeras ediciones de Shakespeare.

下院議員の事務所を収容する三棟の
下院オフィスビルディングの一つ。
上院議員が事務所を置く二棟の
上院オフィスビルディングの一つ。どの
オフィスビルディングも国会議事堂と地下道
システムで便利に結ばれている。
フォルガー・シェークスピア図書館には
シェークスピアの初期の版を集めた世界最大の
コレクションが収められている。

ose to the Capitol are the Department of Labor, the
epartment of Health and Human Services, and the Taft
emorial.

eben dem Capitol befinden sich das Arbeitsministerium,
as Ministerium für Gesundheitswesen und
enschendienste und das Taft-Denkmal.

Non loin du Capitole, on trouve aussi le Ministère du Travail,
le Ministère de la Santé et des Services Sociaux et le
Mémorial Taft.

Cerca del Capitol se encuentra el Ministerio del Trabajo, el
Ministerio de la Sanidad y de los Servicios Humanos y el
Monumento Taft.

国会議事堂の近くにある労働省、保険省、
タフト記念碑。

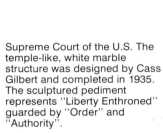

Supreme Court of the U.S. The temple-like, white marble structure was designed by Cass Gilbert and completed in 1935. The sculptured pediment represents "Liberty Enthroned" guarded by "Order" and "Authority".

La Cour Suprême des Etats-Unis. La construction en marbre a la forme d'un temple; elle fut dessinée par Cass Gilbert et achevée en 1935. Le fronton sculpté représente "Liberté sur Trône" protégée par "Ordre" et "Autorité".

Der Oberste Gerichtshof der Vereinigten Staaten. Diese tempelähnliche Architektur aus weißem Marmor wurde von Cass Gilbert entworfen und im Jahre 1935 fertiggestellt. Der gemeißelte Giebel stellt die "Freiheit auf dem Throne dar", die von der "Ordnung" und der "Autorität" bewacht wird.

La Corte Suprema de los Estados Unidos. El edificio con forma de templo, con estructura de mármol, fue diseñado por Cass Gilbert y completado en 1935. El frontón esculpido representa a la "Libertad Entronada" vigilada por el "Orden" y por la "Autoridad".

合衆国最高裁判所。
神殿風の白大理石の建物の設計者は
カス・ギルバートで、1935年に
完成した。
ペディメントの彫刻には『秩序』と
『権威』に守られた
『玉座につく自由像』が表されている。

Library of Congress. The Library of Congress was established in 1800, and originally was located in the Capitol. The present massive building was completed in 1897 and shows the influence of the French Renaissance. It is completely decorated with excellent examples of 19th Century art.

Die Kongreßbibliothek. Die Kongreßbibliothek wurde im Jahr 1800 eingerichtet und war ursrünglich im Kapitol untergebracht. Das derzeitige massive Gebäude wurde im Jahre 1897 fertiggestellt und spiegelt den Einfluß der französischen Renaissance wider. Es ist zur Gänze mit hervorragenden Kunstwerken aus dem neunzehnten Jahrhundert geschmückt.

La bibliothèque du Congrès. La bibliothèque du Congrès fut fondée en 1800; elle avait été installée, à l'origine, dans le Capitole. La construction actuelle, massive, fut achevée en 1897 et évoque l'influence de la Renaissance Française. Elle est entièrement décorée d'oeuvres d'art datant du XIXème siècle.

Biblioteca del Congreso. La Biblioteca del Congreso fue establecida en 1800, y originariamente estaba situada en el Capitolio. El imponente edificio actual fue completado en 1897 y muestra la influencia del Renacimento Francés. Está completamente decorado con excelentes ejemplares del arte del siglo XIX.

国会図書館。1800年に設立された
国会図書館はもともと国会議事堂の中にあった。
現在のどっしりした建物は1897年に完成し、
フランス・ルネッサンスの影響が見られる。
全面にすばらしい19世紀美術の装飾が
施されている。

In the Botanical Gardens there are regular and changing displays which correspond to the seasons of the year.

Dans les Jardins Botaniques ont lieu régulièrement des expositions variées, expositions correspondant aux différentes saisons de l'année.

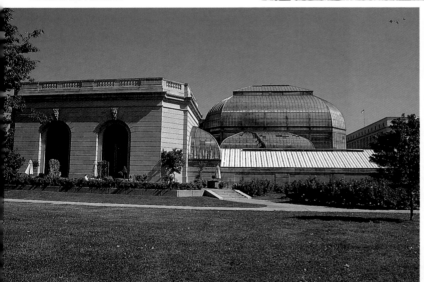

In den Botanischen Gärten finden der Saison entsprechende regelmäßige und verschiedenartige Blumenausstellungen statt.

En los Jardines Botánicos hay exposiciones periódicas y variadas que corresponden a las estaciones del año.

植物園の中のディスプレーは季節に応じて常に変化している。

The Ulysses S. Grant Memorial at the West side of the Capitol.

Le Mémorial d'Ulysses S. Grant sur le côté ouest du Capitole.

Das Ulysses S. Grant Memorial an der Westseite des Kapitols.

Al oeste del Capitolio se encuentra el Monumento Ulysses S. Grant.

国会議事堂の西側にあるユリシーズ・S・グラント記念碑。

The National Air and Space Museum is dedicated to human's adventure in the conquest of air and space. The Permanent Exhibit contains the ''Spirit of St. Louis'' and the first rockets traveling into space.

Le Musée de l'Aviation et de l'Espace est consacré à la conquête des airs et de l'espace par l'être humain. L'exposition permanente présente le ''Spirit of St. Louis'' et les premières fusées lancées dans l'espace.

Das Nationale Luft- und Raumfahrtsmuseum ist dem Abenteuer des Menschen bei der Eroberung von Luft und Raum gewidmet. Die ständige Ausstellung zeigt den ''Spirit of St. Louis'' und die ersten Raumfahrtraketen.

El Museo Nacional Aeronáutica y del Espacio está dedicado a las aventuras del hombre en la conquista del cielo y del espacio. La Exposición Permanente exhibe el ''Spirit of St. Louis'' y los primeros cohetes mandados al espacio.

空と宇宙の征服を目指す人間の冒険に捧げられた
国立航空宇宙博物館。スピリット・オブ・セント・ルイス号、
宇宙を飛んだ最初のロケットなどが常設展示されている。

ithsonian ''Castle''. The Smithsonian institution, ngly called ''the nation's attic'' was founded in 46 under the terms of the will of James ithson, an English scientist who had never ssed the Atlantic.

Smithsonian ''Castle'' (Château Smithsonien). L'institution Smithsonienne, appelée affectueusement ''mansarde de la Nation'', fut fondée en 1846 conformément au testament de James Smithson, un savant Anglais qui n'avait jamais traversé l'Atlantique.

Die Smithsonische ''Burg''. Das Smithsonische Institut, in liebenswerter Weise auch die ''Mansarde der Nation'' genannt, wurde im Jahre 1846 dem letzten Willen von James Smithson entsprechend gegründet. Smithson war ein englischer Wissenschaftler, der selbst niemals den Atlantik überquert hatte.

El ''Castillo'' Smithsoniano. La Institución Smithsoniana, cariñosamente llamada ''el ático de la nación'', fue fundada en 1846 conformemente con la voluntad de James Smithson, un científico inglés que nunca había cruzado el Atlántico.

スミソニアン城。 〈国の屋根裏部屋〉という 愛称で親しまれる スミソニアン協会はついに 一度も大西洋を渡ることが なかったイギリス人科学者 ジェームズ・スミソンの 意志によって１８４６年に 設立された。

The aerial view shows the Smithsonian Institution's main buildings. The Arts and Industries Building, the Hirshhorn Museum, the Air and Space Museum, and the Castle.

Diese Luftaufnahme zeigt die Hauptgebäude der Smithsonian Institution, das Arts and Industries Building, das Hishhorn Museum, das Luft-und Raumfahrtsmuseum und das Schloss.

Vue aérienne des principaux immeubles de l'Institut Smithsonien. L'immeuble des Arts et de l'Industrie, le Musée Hirshhron, le Musée de l'Aviation et de l'Espace et le Château.

La vista aérea muestra los principales edificios de la Institución Smithsoniana, el Edificio de Arte e Industria, el Museo Hirshhorn, el Museo de Aeronáutica y del Espacio y el Castillo.

スミソニアン協会の主な建物の空からの眺め。
芸術産業ビルディング、ハーシュホーン博物館、
航空宇宙博物館、そして城が見える。

...e Arts and Industries Building and the Museum of ...rican Art.

...as Arts and Industries Buildung und das Museum ...rikanischer Kunst.

L'immeuble des Arts et de l'Industrie et le Musée de l'Art Africain.

El Edificio de Arte e Industria y el Museo de Arte Africano.

芸術産業ビルディングとアフリカン・アート
美術館。

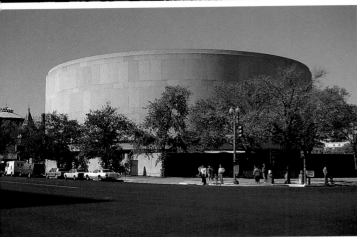
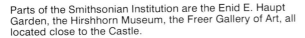

Parts of the Smithsonian Institution are the Enid E. Haupt Garden, the Hirshhorn Museum, the Freer Gallery of Art, all located close to the Castle.

Zur Smithsonian Institution gehören der Enid E. Haupt Garden, das Hirshhorn Museum, die Freer Galery of Art, die alle in der Nähe des Schlosses liegen.

Vue partielle de l'Institut Smithsonien: le Jardin Enid E. Haupt, le Musée Hirshhorn, la Galerie d'Art Freer, tous situés non loin du Château.

El Jardín Enid E. Haupt, el Museo Hirshhorn y La Galería de Arte Freer forman parte de la Institución Smithoniana, todos situados cerca del castillo.

スミソニアン協会の一部となっている
エニッド・E・ハウプト庭園、ハーシュホーン博物館、
フリーアー美術館。みな城の近くにある。

The Department of Agriculture and the Bureau of Engraving and Printing, as well as the Holocaust Museum, are located on the South side ot the Mall.

Le Ministère de l'Agriculture et le Bureau de la Sculpture et de la Peinture, tout comme le Musée de l'Holocauste, se trouvent au sud du Mall.

Das Ministerium für Land- und Forstwirtschaft und das Bureau of Engraving and Printing sowie das Holocaust Museum liegen an der Südseite des Mall.

El Ministerio de Agricultura y la Oficina de Impresión y Tipografía, así como el Museo Holocaust se encuentran en el lado sur del Mall.

モールの南にある農業省、印刷局、そして
ホロコースト博物館。

A beautiful aerial view of the Mall shows the N.A.S.A. Building, the Natural History Museum, the National Gallery of Art, and the National Archives. The picture on the bottom left shows the east wing of the National Gallery of Art; pictures on the right page, the Navy Memorial on Pennsylvania Avenue.

Splendide vue aérienne du Mall: l'immeuble de la N.A.S.A., le Musée d'Histoire Naturelle, la Galerie Nationale d'Art et les Archives Nationales. La photo en bas à gauche représente l'aile Est de la Galerie Nationale d'Art; les photos sur la page de droite représentent le Mémorial de la Marine sur Pennsylvania Avenue.

モールの空からの美しい眺め。ＮＡＳＡ
（国家航空宇宙局）の建物、自然史博物館、
国立美術館、国立公文書館が見える。
左下の写真は国立美術館の東翼。
右ページはペンシルベニア・アヴェニューにある
海軍記念碑。

Diese wunderschöne Luftaufnahme des Mall zeigt das N.A.S.A. Building, das naturwissenschaftliche Museum, die National Gallery of Art und die Nationalarchive. Die Abbildung unten links zeigt den Ostflügel der National Gallery of Art; Abbildungen auf der rechten Seite, das Navy Memorial an der Pennsylvania Avenue.

Una heromosa vista aérea del Mall muestra el Edificio N.A.S.A, El Museo de Historia Natural, La Galería Nacional de Arte y el El Archivo Nacional. La imagen en el extremo inferior izquierdo muestra el ala este de la Galería Nacional de Arte; en la página derecha, el Monumento a la Armada en la Avenida Pennsylvania.

The National Archives is the final repository for the permanent records of the U.S. Government. The picture on this page on top shows the National Gallery of Art, on the bottom the Museum of Natural History.

Tous les documents officiels du Gouvernement américain sont conservés aux archives Nationales. La photo du haut représente la Galerie Nationale d'Art, celle du bas le Musée d'Histoire Naturelle.

Die Nationalarchive sind der endgültige Verwahrungsort für Dokumente der amerikanischen Regierung. Das Bild oben auf dieser Seite zeigt die National Gallery of Art, unten das naturwissenschaftliche Museum.

El Archivo Nacional es el depósito final de los registros del Gobierno de los Estados Unidos. La imagen de esta página muestra arriba la Galería Nacional de Arte, abajo el Museo de Historia Natural.

国立公文書館には合衆国政府の公式記録が永久に
保存されている。このページ上の写真は国立美術館、
下は自然史博物館。

Historic Union Station, designed by D.H. Burnham and completed in 1908, the architecture is Roman Classic. The front plaza is dedicated by a memorial to Christopher Columbus. Also pictured above are the Justice Department and the I.R.S. Building. The concourse is the largest room in the world, - 750 ft long and 130 ft wide.

Historic Union Station, das von von D.H. Burnham entworfene und 1908 beendete Gebäude ist in römisch-klassischem Stil gehalten. Der davorliegende Platz ist mit einem ihn darstellenden Denkmal Christoph Kolumbus gewidmet. Photos darunter zeigen das Justizministerium und das I.R.S. Building. Das "Concourse" ist das größte Zimmer der Welt, es ist 750 Fuß lang und 130 breit.

Historic Union Station, dessiné par D.H. Burnham et terminé en 1908, ce bâtiment a été construit dans un style roman classique. Sur le parvis, on peut admirer le mémorial de Christophe Colomb. Les photos du haut représentent le Ministère de la Justice et l'immeuble I.R.S. Avec ses 750 pieds de long et ses 130 pieds de large, le "concourse" est la pièce la plus grande du monde.

Estación Histórica Union, proyectada por D.H. Burnham y terminada en 1908, su arquitectura es clásica romana. La plaza de enfrente está dedicada a la memoria de Cristobal Colón, también en la imagen inferior el Ministerio de Justicia y el Edificio I.R.S. El "concourse" es la habitación más grande del mundo, con un largo y un ancho de 750 y 130 pies respectivamente.

Ｄ・Ｈ・バーナムの設計により１９０８年に完成した ローマ古典主義建築のヒストリック・ユニオン駅。 駅前の広場にはクリストファー・コロンブスに捧げられた 記念碑が立っている。下の写真は司法省とＩＲＳ（国税庁） ビルディング。長さ７５０フィート、幅１３０フィートの 駅のコンコースは世界最大である。

The Department of Labor, the Museum of American History, and the National Gallery of Art.

Le Ministère du Travail, le Musée de l'Histoire Américaine, et la National Gallery of Art.

Das Arbeitsministerium, das Museum für amerikanische Geschichte und die National Gallery of Art.

El Ministerio del Trabajo, el Museo de la Historia Americana y la National Gallery of Art.

労働省、アメリカ史博物館、国立美術館。

Washington Monument. Construction of the Monument was begun in 1848 and was completed in 1884, 85 years after the death of Washington in 1799. The white marble shaft rises 555 feet and stands on the Mall, between the Lincoln Memorial and the Capitol.

Monument à Washington. La construction du Monument commença en 1848 et fut achevée en 1884, 85 ans après la mort de Washington en 1799. La colonne en marbre blanc s'élève à une hauteur de 555 pieds et se dresse sur le Mall entre le Mémorial et le Capitole.

Das Washington-Monument. Die Errichtung dieses gigantischen Denkmals wurde im Jahre 1848 begonnen und 1884 fertiggestellt - 85 Jahre nach dem Tod von George Washington im Jahre 1799. Der weiße Marmorobelisk erreichte eine Höhe von 555 Fuß und befindet sich am Mall zwischen der Lincoln-Gedächtnisstätte und dem Kapitol.

Monumento a Washington. La construcción del Monumento se comenzó en 1848 y fué completada en 1884, 85 años después de la muerte de Washington en 1799. La columna de mármol blanco alcanza los 555 pies y está situada sobre el Mall, entre el monumento a la memoria de Lincoln y el Capitolio.

ワシントン記念塔。塔の建設は１８４８年に始められ、１７９９年に亡くなったワシントンの没後８５年の１８８４年に完成した。白い大理石の方尖塔の高さは５５５フィートで、モールのリンカーン記念館と国会議事堂の間に立っている。

The Washington Monument is the most prominent and visible structure on the skyline of the nation's capital. The Washington National Monument Society was organized in 1833 to erect a monument; however the cornerstone was not laid until 1848 and it was not open to the public until 1888.

Le Monument à George Washington est la construction la plus haute et donc la plus visible de toute la capitale. En 1833, la Société pour le Monument National à Washington fut fondée pour ériger le dit monument; toutefois, la première pierre ne fut posée qu'en 1848 et le public ne pût admirer l'oeuvre terminée qu'en 1888.

Das Washington Monument ist das markanteste und auffallendste Gebäude an der Skyline der Hauptstadt. Die Washington National Monument Society wurde 1833 mit dem Ziel gegründet, ein entsprechendes Monument zu errichten, doch der Grundstein wurde nicht vor 1848 gelegt und erst 1888 wurde es für den Publikumsbesuch freigegeben.

El Monumento a Washington es la construcción más prominente y visible de la línea de rascacielos de la capital de Estados Unidos. La Washington National Monument Society fue organizada en 1833 para construir un monumento; sin embargo la primera piedra fue colocada solo en 1848 y se abrió al público solo en 1888.

スカイラインに一際高くそびえるワシントン記念塔は首都で
もっとも目につく建造物である。記念塔建設を目的とする
ワシントン国立記念塔協会は１８３３年に設立されたが、
塔の定礎式は１８４８年まで行われず、一般に公開されたのは
１８８８年のことである。

Along Constitution Avenue lies the National Academy of Sciences & Engineering. A statue of Albert Einstein commemorates the achievements of this great scientist.

Sur Constitution Avenue se dresse l'Académie Nationale des Sciences & de l'Ingénierie. La statue d'Albert Einstein commémore l'oeuvre de ce chercheur de génie.

Entlang der Constitution Avenue liegt die National Academy of Sciences & Engineering. Eine Statue Albert Einsteins erinnert an die Leistungen dieses grossen Wissenschaftlers.

A lo largo de la Avenida Constitution se encuentra la Academia Nacional de Ciencias y Ingeniería. Una Estatua de Albert Einstein conmemora los logros de este gran científico.

コンスティテューション・アヴェニュー沿いに
ある国立科学技術アカデミー。アルバート・
アインシュタインの偉業を記念して、
この偉大な科学者の像が立っている。

The Department of Interior, the Federal Reserve Board, and the F.B.I. Building. The Old Post Office has been a popular shopping and dining center since its conversion.

Le Ministère de l'Intérieur, la Réserve Fédérale et l'immeuble du F.B.I. La vieille Poste a été transformée en un centre commercial et de restauration très animé.

Das Innenministerium, der Zentralbankrat und das F.B.I. Building. Aus dem alten Postamt ist seit seines Umbaus ein populäres Shopping- und Dinner-Center geworden.

El Ministerio del Interior, el Federal Reserve Board y el Edificio del F.B.I. La vieja Oficina de Correo ha sido a partir de su transformación un centro comercial y de restaurantes muy popular.

内務省、連邦準備制度理事会、FBI（連邦捜査局）の建物。
旧郵便局は現在人気のあるショッピングと食事のセンターとなっている。

The Vietnam Memorial is dedicated to the 58,132 men and women who died in service related to the Vietnam War. The Memorial, on the National Mall near the Lincoln Memorial, was dedicated in 1982. It is not the traditional white marble tribute but consists of two highly polished granite walls that meet to form a "V".

Le "Vietnam Memorial" est dédié aux 58 132 hommes et femmes morts durant la guerre du Vietnam. Le monument, situé sur National Avenue, près du Mémorial de Lincoln, fut inauguré en 1982. Contrairement aux monuments traditionnels en marbre blanc, celui-ci consiste en deux colonnes de granit formant un "V".

Das Vietnam Memorial ist den 58.132 Männern und Frauen gewidmet, die im Vietnamkrieg gefallen sind. Das Denkmal am National Mall in der Nähe des Lincoln Memorials wurde 1982 eingeweiht. Es handelt sich hierbei nicht um die übliche Huldigung aus weissem Marmor, sondern um zwei Hochglanz-Granitblöcke, die ein "V" bilden.

El Monumento a Vietnam está dedicado a los 58.132 hombres y mujeres que murieron dando servicio en la Guerra de Vietnam. El Monumento, en el National Mall cerca del Monumento a Lincoln, fue inaugurado en 1982. No es la típica lápida tradicional de mármol blanco sino son dos paredes extremadamente brillantes de granito que se encuentran formando una "V".

ヴェトナム戦争で死亡した
５万８１３２人の男女に捧げられた
ヴェトナム記念碑。１９８２年に
リンカーン記念館近くの
ナショナル・モールに建設された。
伝統的な白大理石ではなく、
Ｖ字型に交わる二枚の磨き花崗岩で
作られている。

The memorial to the 16th President, Abraham Lincoln, is a white marble building of classic design, resembling the Parthenon of Greece. It was designed by Henry Bacon and completed in 1922. Facing the Lincoln Memorial on the West side are these massive statues given to the people of the United States by the people of Italy.

Le Mémorial au 16ème Président, Abraham Lincoln, est un édifice en marbre blanc de style classique, qui rappelle le Parthénon grec. Il fut conçu par Henry Bacon et achevé en 1922. En face du Mémorial à Lincoln, à l'ouest, se trouvent des statues massives, don du peuple italien au peuple américain.

Das Denkmal, unserm 16. Präsidenten Abraham Lincoln gewidmet, ist ein weißes Marmorgebäude in klassischer Linienführung und erinnert uns an das Parthenon von Griechenland. Die Entwürfe stammen von Henry Bacon; der Bau wurde im Jahre 1922 beendet. Die massiven Steinstatuen, die der Lincoln-Gedächtnisstätte an der Westseite gegenüberstehen, sind der amerikanischen Bevölkerung vom italienischen Volk geschenkt worden.

El monumento a la memoria del nuestro decimosexto Presidente, Abraham Lincoln, es un edificio de mármol blanco de diseño clásico parecido al Partenón de Grecia. Fue diseñado por Henry Bacon y completado en 1922. En frente del Monumento a Lincoln en la parte oeste se encuentran las imponentes estatuas regaladas al pueblo de los Estados Unidos por el pueblo de Italia.

第十六代大統領アブラハム・リンカーンの記念館はアテネのパンテオンを思わせる古典様式の白大理石の建物である。ヘンリー・ベーコンの設計で１９２２年に完成した。リンカーン記念館の西側外壁はイタリア国民から合衆国国民に贈られた堂々たる彫刻で飾られている。

Lincoln Memorial. This 19-foot-high marble
statue of the seated Lincoln was executed
by Daniel Chester French and is located
inside the Memorial. Inscribed above the
statue are the words:

IN THIS TEMPLE
AS IN THE HEARTS OF THE PEOPLE
FOR WHOM HE SAVED THE UNION
THE MEMORY OF ABRAHAM LINCOLN
IS ENSHRINED FOREVER

Mémorial à Lincoln. Cette statue en marbre
de 19 pieds de hauteur, représentant
Lincoln assis, fut réalisée par Daniel
Chester French; elle se trouve à l'intérieur
du Mémorial. On peut lire au-dessus de la
statue:

DANS CE TEMPLE
COMME DANS LES COEURS DES HOMMES
POUR LESQUELS IL SAUVA L'UNION
LE SOUVENIR D'ABRAHAM LINCOLN
RESTE A TOUT JAMAIS GRAVÉ.

Die Lincoln-Gedächtnisstätte. Diese 19 Fuß
hohe Marmorstatue zeigt den sitzenden
Präsidenten Lincoln; sie wurde von Daniel
Chester French gemeißelt und im Innere
des Monuments aufgestellt. Über der
Statue sind folgende Worte auf einer
Inschrifttafel graviert:

IN DIESEM TEMPEL
WIE IN DEN HERZEN DER MENSCHEN
UM DERENTWILLEN ER DIE
UNION GERETTET HAT.
IST DAS ANDENKEN AN ABRAHAN LINCOLN
FÜR EWIG FESTGEHALTEN.

Monumento a la Memoria de Lincoln. Esta estatua de Mármol de 19 pies de altura que representa a Lincoln sentado, fue realizada por Daniel Cheste French y está situada dentro del Memorial. Sobre la estatua están grabadas las siguientes palabras:

EN ESTE TEMPLO
COMO EN LOS CORAZONES DE LA
PERSONAS
PARA LAS CUALES SALVÓ A LA UNION
EL RECUERDO DE ABRAHAM LINCOLN
SE CONSERVA COMO UNA RELIQUIA
PARA SIEMPRE

リンカーン記念館。大理石で作られた
高さ19フィートのリンカーン座像は
ダニエル・チェスター・フレンチの作で、
記念館の内部に置かれ、像の上には
次の言葉が刻まれている。
　　人民のために合衆国を救った
　アブラハム・リンカーンの思い出は
　　　人々の心の中と同様
　　　　この神殿の中に
　　　永遠に留められる。

The Korean War Memorial shows a series of statues of soldiers marching in full battle gear. It was designed by Cooper-Lecky Architects, with Frank Gaylord III as sculptor, and Louis Nelson Associates as muralist.

Le Korean War Memorial abrite une série de statues de soldats en uniforme de combat. Projeté par Cooper-Lecky Architects, les sculptures sont l'oeuvre de Frank Gaylord III et les peintures murales de Louis Nelson Associates.

Das Koreanische Kriegsmemorial zeigt mehrere Statuen von in voller Kampfausrüstung marschierenden Soldaten. Es wurde von Cooper-Lecky Architects entworfen, mit Frank Gaylord III. als Bildhauer und Louis Nelson Associates zur Mauerverzierung.

El Korean War Memorial tiene una serie de estatuas de soldados que marchan vestidos con uniforme de guerra. El proyecto ha sido realizado por Cooper-Lecky Architects; las esculturas son de Frank Gaylord III y los murales de Louis Nelsen Associates.

朝鮮戦争記念碑は、まさに戦闘態勢にある軍隊の行進像である。これは建築家クーパー・レッキー設計、フランク・ゲイロルド３世彫刻、ルイ・ネルソン社施工による作品である。

Franklin Delano Roosevelt Memorial has a building dedicated to each of the four terms the President served. It opened in 1997. The sculptor of the seated FDR and Fala is Neil Estern, while the stone cutter for the inscription is John Benson.

Le Franklin Delano Roosevelt Memorial est constitué d'un bâtiment dédié aux quatre mandats du Président. Il a été inauguré en 1997. La statue de FDR assis et Fala est l'oeuvre du sculpteur Neil Estern alors que l'inscription a été réalisée par John Benson.

Das Franklin Delano Roosevelt Memorial hat ein Gebäude, das jeweils den vier Amtszeiten gewidmet ist, während welcher der Präsident das Amt innehatte. Es wurde 1997 eröffnet. Der Bildhauer des sitzenden FDR und Falas ist Neil Estern, während der Steinmetze für die Inschriften John Benson ist.

El Franklin Delano Roosevelt Memorial tiene un edificio dedicado a cada uno de los cuatro periodos en los que el Presidente estuvo en el cargo. Ha sido inaugurado en 1997. El escultor de FDR sentado y Fala es Neil Estern, mientras que el picapedrero que ha realizado la inscripción es John Benson.

1997年に落成したルーズベルト大統領の記念碑は、大統領任期を四つに分けて描いている。椅子に座ったルーズベルトと愛犬ファラの像はネイル・エスターン作、碑銘彫刻はジョン・ベンソンによるものである。

The Commerce Department, the Treasury Department and the Second Army Division Memorial are located near the White House.

Le Ministère du Commerce, le Ministère du Trésor et le Mémorial de la Seconde Division Armée se trouvent non loin de la Maison Blanche.

Das Handelsministerium, das Schatzministerium und das Second Army Division Memorial liegen in der Nähe des Weißen Hauses.

El Ministerio de Comercio, el Ministerio del Tesoro y el Monumento a la Segunda División de la Armada se encuentran cerca de la Casa Blanca.

ホワイトハウスの近くにある商業省、財務省、陸軍第二師団記念碑。

This distinctive domed building houses a 19 foot high statue of our third President of the United States and the author of the Declaration of Independence. Domes on buildings were favored by Jefferson, himself an architect. Above the entrance which faces the Tidal Basin, is a sculpture which depicts Jefferson standing before the committee appointed by the Continental Congress to write the Declaration of Independence. There are four panels on the interior walls which are engraved with writings of the third President. Surrounding the Memorial are the famous Oriental Cherry Trees. When they are in bloom in early April, thousands of visitors come to see the beautiful blossoms during the ''Cherry Blossom Festival''. The memorial is open at all times.

Cet édifice majestueux à coupole abrite une statue de 19 pieds de haut figurant le Président des Etats Unis et l'auteur de la Déclaration d'Indépendance. Les coupoles qui surplombent les édifices ont été édifiées sous l'égide de Jefferson en personne, qui était aussi architecte. Au-dessus de l'entrée, qui donne sur le Tidal Basin, on peut admirer une sculpture en pied de Jefferson devant le Comité chargé par le Congrès Continental de rédiger la Déclaration d'Indépendance. A l'intérieur, les écritures gravées sur les murs sont l'oeuvre du troisième Président des Etats Unis. Le Mémorial est entouré des célèbres Cerisiers Orientaux. En avril, lorsqu'ils sont en fleur, des milliers de visiteurs viennent admirer ce magnifique spectacle de la nature à l'occasion du ''Festival du Cerisier en Fleur''. Le Mémorial est ouvert en permanence.

In diesem bedeutenden Gebäude mit Kuppelgewölbe befindet sich die 19 Fuß hohe Statue des dritten Präsidenten der Vereinigten Staaten und Verfasser der Unabhängigkeitserklärung. Jefferson, der auch Architekt war, förderte den Bau der Gebäudekuppeln. Über dem Eingang, der auf den Tidal Basin blickt, befindet sich eine Skulptur, die Jefferson vor dem Komitee darstellt, das vom Kontinentalkongreß mit der Verfassung der Unabhängigkeitserklärung beauftragt wurde. An den Innenwänden hängen vier Tafeln, in denen die Schriften des dritten Präsidenten eingraviert sind. Um das Denkmal sehen Sie die berühmten Orientalischen Kirschbäumen. Im April, wenn sie blühen, bewundern Tausende von Besuchern diese wunderschönen Blüten anläßlich des ''Festivals des blühenden Kirschbaumes''. Das Gebäude ist immer geöffnet.

Este gran edificio con cúpula aloja en su interior una estatua de 19 pies del tercer Presidente de los Estados Unidos, autor de la Declarción de la Independencia. Las cúpulas sobres los edificios fueron promovidas por Jefferson mismo, él también arquitecto. Arriba de la entrada que mira hacia el Tidal Basin se encuentra una escultura que representa Jefferson de pie ante la Junta encargada por el Congreso Continental de la redacción de la Declaración de la Independencia. Posee cuatro paneles sobre las paredes internas grabadas con los escritos del tercer Presidente. Alrededor del edificio conmemorativo encontramos los famosos Cerezos Orientales. Cuando florecen en abril, millares de visitantes vienen a ver estas maravillosas flores en ocasión del ''Festibal del Cerezo en Flor''. El edificio a la memoria está siempre abierto.

人目を引くドーム型屋根の建物には、独立宣言の
起草者である第三代大統領ジェファーソンの
高さ１９フィートに及ぶ巨大な彫像が収められている。
ドームは建築家でもあった大統領が好んだ様式だった。
タイダル・ベイスン（係船ドック）に面した正面玄関の
上には、大陸会議から独立宣言を起草するように
任命された委員会に出席するジェファーソンの像がある。
記念館の中に入ると、ジェファーソン自筆の宣言が
彫られた４枚のパネルが壁に掛かっている。
そして建物の周囲には有名な東洋の桜の木がある。
４月初旬にこの桜が満開になると、〈桜祭り〉が催され、
何千人もの人々がこの美しい桜を楽しみにやって来る。
ジェファーソン記念館は年中無休。

Jefferson Memorial. The Memorial, designed by John Russel Pope, was dedicated in 1943. The classic style reflects Jefferson's own taste in architecture and bears a marked resemblance to Monticello, his home in Virginia.

Mémorial Jefferson. Le Monument commémoratif, réalisé par John Russel Pope fut inauguré en 1943. Le style classique reflète le goût architectural de Jefferson lui-même et ressemble beaucoup à Monticello, sa demeure en Virginie.

Das Jefferson-Denkmal. Dieses Denkmal, entworfen von John Russel, wurde im Jahre 1943 eingeweiht. Der klassische Stil entspricht Jeffersons eigenem Geschmack hinsichtlich Architektur und hat in vielem unverkennbare Ähnlichkeiten mit Monticello, seinem Landhaus in Virginia.

Monumento a la memoria de Jefferson. El Monumento, diseñado por John Russel Pope, fué dedicado en 1943. El estilo clásico refleja el proprio gusto de Jefferson en cuanto se refiere a arquitectura y tiene un parecido notable con Monticello, su casa en Virginia.

ジェファーソン記念館。ジョン・ラッセル・ポープ設計のこの記念館は１９４３年に除幕式が行われた。古典的な様式は建築家でもあったジェファーソン自身の趣味で、ヴァージニア州にある彼の邸宅、モンティチェッロにとてもよく似ている。

The South Portico of the White House. The White House was burned by the British in 1814, but was rebuilt and the porticos were added in 1820s.

Le Portique sud de la Maison-Blanche. La Maison-Blanche fut incendiée par les Anglais en 1814 et reconstruite, avec ses portiques, au cours des années 1820.

Der Säulengang an der Südfassade des Weißen Hauses. Das Weiße Haus wurde im Jahre 1814 von den Engländern niedergebrannt, aber in den Zwanzigerjahren des 19. Jahrhunderts wieder aufgebaut und erhielt damals seine Säulengänge.

El Pórtico Sur de la Casa
Blanca. La Casa Blanca fue
incendiada por los Ingleses en
1814, pero fue reconstruida y
se le añadieron los pórticos en
los años 1820.

ホワイトハウスの南側柱廊玄関。
1814年、ホワイトハウスは
イギリス軍によって焼かれたが、
1820年代に再建され、
この柱廊が付け加えられた。

The White House has the simple elegance of a gracious American Home. It reflects the design of manor houses in Ireland, England and France.

La Maison Blanche a l'élégance simple des maisons américaines. Elle rappelle le style des manoirs irlandais, britanniques et français.

Das Weiße Haus hat die schlichte Eleganz eines schönen amerikanischen Heims. Es spiegelt den Stil irischer, englischer und französischer Herrensitze wieder.

La Casa Blanca posee la elegancia simple de una importante casa americana. Refleja la línea de las casas señoriales de Irlanda, Inglaterra y Francia.

ホワイトハウスには上品なアメリカ住宅の簡素な優雅さが備わっている。またアイルランド、イギリス、フランスの貴族邸宅の様式の影響が見られる。

Top picture: Lafayette Park with Jackson Statue.
Below left: Jackson Place with Truxtun-Decatur House.
St. John's Church

Photo en haut: Parc Lafayette et Statue de Jackson.
En bas à gauche: Jackson et Truxtun-Decatur House.
Eglise St. John

Bild oben: Der Lafayette-Park mit der Jackson-Statue.
Unten links: Jackson Place mit dem Truxtun-Decatur House.
St. -John-Kirche.

Ilustración superior: Parque Lafayette con la estatua de Jackson.
Abajo a la izquierda: Jackson Place con Truxtun-Decatur House.
Iglesia de St. John.

上の写真：ラファイエット・パークとジャクソン像。
左下より：ジャクソン広場とトラスタン・
ドゥカトゥール・ハウス。セント・ジョン教会。

Top, the Renwick Gallery, bottom, American Red Cross Building.
Next page, the OAS Building, the Blair-Lee House, official "Guest House" of the U.S.; the Constitution Hall, D.A.R.; the Corcoran Gallery of Art. Exhibits include old masters, contemporary works and antique furnishings.

En haut: la Galerie Renwick; en bas: les bureaux de la Croix-Rouge américaine. Page suivante: les bureaux de l'OAS, la maison Blair-Lee, et la "Guest House" officielle des Etats-Unis; le Hall de la Constitution, D.A.R.; la Galerie d'Art Corcoran. On peut y admirer des chefs-d'oeuvre anciens et contemporains et du mobilier antique.

Oben, die Renwick Gallery, unten, das amerikanische Rote Kreuz Gebäude. Auf der nächsten Seite, das OAS Building, das Blair-Lee House, offizielles "Gästehaus" der Vereinigten Staaten; die Constitutional Hall; D.A.R.; die Corcoran Kunstgalerie. Die Exponate umfassen alte Meister, zeitgenössische Kunst und antike Möbel.

Arriba, la Galería Renwick, abajo, el Edificio de la Cruz Roja Americana. Página siguiente, el Edificio OAS. La Casa Blair-Lee, la "Guest House" (casa de invitados) oficial de los Estados Unidos; el Edificio Constitution, D.A.R.; la Galería de Arte Corcoran, la exposición incluye, obras de antiguos maestros, obras contemporáneas y antiguos mobiliarios.

上：レンウィック・ギャラリー。
下：米国赤十字協会本部
次ページ：ＯＡＳ（米州機構）本部。合衆国の
公式〈迎賓館〉のブレア・リー・ハウス。
憲法会館、ＤＡＲ（米国愛国婦人会）。
歴史的な名作や現代美術、アンティック家具などを
展示するコーコラン美術館。

ISABEL LA CATOLICA
REINA DE CASTILLA

This side top, the National Portrait Gallery; bottom, the U.S. Court of Claims; large picture, the First U.S. Army Division Memorial.

Sur le côté en haut: La Galerie Nationale des Portraits; en bas: la Cour de Justice Américaine; grande photo: le Mémorial de la Première Division Armée des Etats-Unis.

Auf dieser Seite oben, die National Portrait Gallery; unten, der amerikanische Gerichtshof; grosses Photo, das First U.S. Army Division Memorial.

De este lado arriba, la National Portrait Gallery; abajo, la Corte de Apelación de los Estados Unidos; imagen grande, el Monumento a la Primera Division de la Armada de los Estados Unidos.

上は国立ポートレート・ギャラリー。下は合衆国請求裁判所。
大きい写真は合衆国陸軍第一師団記念碑。

The entire Treasury Building covers five acres. It is built in a Greek Revival style with walls of granite. The existing building is the third one built on the site. The previous two were destroyed by fire. All the area bounding the building is Washington's financial district.

Les bureaux du Ministère du Trésor s'étendent sur cinq acres (soit plus de 20.000 m2). L'immeuble fut construit dans un style qui rappelle celui des temples grecs avec des blocs de granit. L'actuel immeuble est le troisième du nom. Les deux premiers furent détruits par les flammes. Toute la zone alentour n'est autre que le quartier financier de Washington.

Das gesamte Gebäude des Schatzamtes erstreckt sich über fünf Acre. Es wurde in griechischem Stil mit Mauern aus Granit erbaut. Das jetzige Gebäude ist das dritte, das an dieser Stelle errichtet wurde. Die beiden früheren Gebäude fielen einem Brand zu Opfer. Das Gebiet rund um das Gebäude ist Washingtons Finanzdistrikt.

El entero Edificio del Tesoro cubre cinco acres. Está construído con un estilo griego con paredes de granito. El edificio existente es el tercero construído en el lugar. Los dos anteriores fueron destruídos por incendios. Toda la zona que rodea el edificio constituye el distrito financiero de Washington.

財務省本部は5エーカー
（2万平方メートル以上）もの
広大な敷地を占めている。
古代ギリシャの復活様式で、
壁は花崗岩である。
二度も火災にあって全焼し、
現在の建物は三番目のもの。
周辺の地域はワシントンの
金融街となっている。

Top, Pleasure boats at the Washington Channel; right, the National Zoological Park; bottom, 12th Street and Constitution Avenue, showing the tower of the ''Old Post Office''.

En haut, des bateaux naviguent dans le Canal de Washington; à droite, le Parc Zoologique National; en bas: 12th Street et Constitution Avenue, figurant la tour du ''Vieux Bureau de Poste''.

Oben: Boote im Washingtoner Kanal; rechts: der Nationale Zoologische Garten; unten die 12th street und die Constitution Avenue mit dem Turm des ''Alten Postamtes''.

Arriba, barcas en el canal de Washington; a la derecha, el Jardín Zoológico Nacional; abajo, 12th Street y Constitution Avenue, ilustrando la torre de la ''Vieja Oficina Postal''.

上：ワシントン運河の遊覧船。右：ワシントン国立動物園。
下：１２番街とコンスティテューション・アヴェニュー。
〈旧郵便局〉の塔が見える。

Théâtre Ford/Musée Lincoln; l'endroit où le président Lincoln fut assassiné a été restauré et l'on a recréé la scène où eu lieu le tragique événement. En face du théâtre se dresse la Maison de Petersen et, à quelques îlots, le quartier chinois de Washington.

d's Theater/Lincoln Museum, where President Lincoln s assassinated, has been restored to re-create the ting where this tragic event occurred. Across from the ater is the Petersen House, and just a few blocks away, shington's China Town.

Ford's Theater/Lincoln Museum, wo Präsident Lincoln ermordet wurde, wurde wiederhergestellt, um den Schauplatz nachzustellen, an dem dieses tragische Ereignis stattfand. Gegenüber dem Theater liegen das Petersen House und ein paar Häuserblocks weiter China Town, Washingtons chinesisches Viertel.

ォード劇場／リンカーン博物館。リンカーン大統領が
殺されたこの劇場は、悲劇が起こった当時の模様を
現するために改装された。劇場の向かいにあるのは
ーターソン・ハウス。数ブロック先にワシントンの
ャイナ・タウンがある。

El Teatro Ford/Museo Lincoln, donde el Presidente Lincoln fue asesinado ha sido restaurado para recrear el escenario donde se produjo este trágico evento. Al otro lado del Teatro se encuentra la casa Petersen, solo algunas cuadras más allá, la China Town de Washington.

The John F. Kennedy Center for the Performing Arts is located on the banks of the Potomac river. Its facilities include an opera house, a concert hall and two large theaters. Harbour Place lies just west of it, and the Watergate Hotel, east. The Pentagon is the U.S. Defense Department Headquarters. Here the Secretaries of the Army, Navy, Air Force and Coast Guard have offices. More than 23,000 people work here.

Le Centre John F. Kennedy pour les Arts du Spectacle se trouve sur les rives du fleuve Potomac. Il abrite un auditorium, une salle de concerts et deux grands théâtres. Non loin de là, à l'ouest, Harbour Place et, à l'est, l'hôtel Watergate. Le Pentagone est le quartier général du Ministère de la Défense des Etats-Unis. Il abrite les bureaux des Secrétaires des Armées, de la Marine, de l'Aviation et de la Garde Côtière. Plus de 23 000 personnes y travaillent.

Das John F. Kenndy Center für darstellende Künste liegt am Ufer des Potomac Flusses. Die Anlage umfasst ein Opernhaus, eine Konzerthalle und zwei grosse Theater. Harbour Place liegt genau westlich und das Watergate Hotel östlich davon. Das Pentagon ist das Hauptquartier des U.S. Verteidigungsministeriums. Hier haben die Heeres-, Kriegsmarine- und Luftwaffenminister und der Küstenwach- und Rettungsdienst ihre Büros. Über 23.000 Menschen sind hier angestellt.

El Centro John F. Kennedy para Representaciones Artísticas se encuentra en las orillas del río Potomac. Sus instalaciones incluyen teatro de ópera, una sala de conciertos y dos grandes teatros. El Harbour Place está ubicado solo al oeste de éste, y el Hotel Watergate, al este. El Pentagon es la Jefatura del Departamento de Defensa de los Estados Unidos. Aquí se encuentran las secretarías del Ejercito, de la Marina, de las Fuerzas Aereas y del Guardia Costera. Aquí trabajan más de 23.000 personas.

ポトマック河畔にある
舞台芸術のジョン・F・
ケネディ・センター。
この中にはオペラ・
ハウス、コンサート・
ホール、そして広い
劇場が二つある。
すぐ西側にはハーバー・
プレース、東側には
ウォーターゲート・
ホテルがある。
ペンタゴンとは
合衆国国防省司令部の
ことである。ここには
陸軍、海軍、空軍、
沿岸警備隊の本部が
あり、2万3千人以上
働いている。

Georgetown, now a part of Washington, was first settled in the 17th century. It has been carefully restored and has become one of the most exclusive residential sections in Washington. Also, located in Georgetown is the prestigious Georgetown University. Washington Cathedral, picture bottom left, officially the Cathedral Church of St. Peter and St. Paul, is the world's sixth largest ecclesiastical edifice. The National Shrine of the Immaculate Conception, picture top left, is the tribute of American Catholics to Our Blessed Mother as Patroness of the Country. Next page, an aerial view of Georgetown.

Georgetown, qui fait maintenant partie de Washington, fut fondée au 17e siècle. Soigneusement restaurée, cette ancienne petite ville est devenue l'un des quartiers résidentiels les plus chics de Washington. On y trouve la prestigieuse Université Georgetown. Photo en bas à gauche: la cathédrale de Washington, officiellement cathédrale St. Pierre et St. Paul, est sixième au box office des plus grandes églises du monde. La photo en haut à gauche représente le Sanctuaire national de l'Immaculée Conception dédié à Notre Dame Patronne du Pays par la communauté catholique américaine. Page suivante: vue aérienne de Georgetown.

Das heute zu Washington gehörende Georgetown wurde im 18. Jahrhundert gegründet. Es ist stilvoll restauriert worden und ist heute eines der exklusivsten Wohngebiete Washingtons. Hier befindet sich auch die berühmte Georgetown Universität. Washington Cathedral, Photo unten links, offiziell Cathedral Church of St. Peter and St. Paul genannt, ist einer der sechs grössten Kirchenbauten der Welt. Der Nationale Shrine of Immaculate Conception, Photo oben links, wurde von den amerikanischen Katholiken unserer Heiligen Jungfrau, der Schutzpatronin des Landes, gewidmet. Auf der nächsten Seite eine Luftaufnahme von Georgetown.

現在はワシントンの一部であるジョージタウンは、17世紀に開拓された。この古い街は慎重に復元され、ワシントンでもっともシックな住宅街になった。またジョージタウンには権威あるジョージタウン大学、ワシントン大聖堂などがある。左下の写真のワシントン大聖堂は正式にはセント・ピーター・アンド・セント・ポール大聖堂といい、教会建築としては世界で六番目に大きい。左上のイマキュレート・コンセプション聖堂はアメリカ・カトリック教会が国の守護聖人としての聖母に捧げたものである。次のページはジョージタウンの空からの眺め。

Georgetown, hoy parte de Washington, fue fundada en el siglo XVII. Esta ha sido cuidadosamente restaurada y se ha vuelto uno de los lugares residenciales más exclusivos de Washington. También se encuentra la prestigiosa Universidad Georgetown. La importante Catedral Washington, imagen inferior izquierda, oficialmente la Iglesia de St. Peter and St. Paul es el sexto más grande edificio ecleciástico del mundo. El Santuario Nacional de la Inmaculada Concepción, imagen superior izquierda, es el tributo de los Americanos Católicos a Nuestra Santa Madre como Patrona del país. Página siguiente, una vista aérea de Georgetown.

Manassas Battlefield is the site of the second battle of Manassas during the Civil War. It is also known as "Bull Run". There is a visitors center where one can learn of the historic events of the property. There are horse trails and picnic tables.

Manassas Battlefield: c'est ici qu'eût lieu la seconde bataille de Manassas pendant la guerre civile. Elle est également connue sous le nom de "Bull Run". A l'intérieur du centre ouvert au public, les visiteurs peuvent venir consulter des archives retraçant l'historique du pays. Un sentier réservé aux promenades à cheval et une aire de pique-nique sont également à leur disposition.

Manassas Battlefield ist der Schauplatz, an dem während des Bürgerkriegs die zweite Schlacht von Manassas stattfand und ist auch als "Bull Run" bekannt. In einem Besucher-Center kann man sich über die geschichtlichen Ereignisse dieser Stätte informieren. Pferdewege und Picknicktische sind ebenfalls vorhanden.

Manassas Battlefield es el lugar de la segunda batalla de Manassas durante la Guerra Civil. Se lo conoce también como el "Bull Run". Existe un centro para visitantes donde se puede conocer los eventos históricos de la propiedad. Hay senderos para andar a caballo y mesas para pic-nic.

マナサスの戦場は南北戦争の際、第二回目のマナサスの
戦いの場となり、〈ブル・ラン〉の名でも知られる。
観光センターでは地元の歴史的なできごとについての
資料を見ることができる。また乗馬用の小道や
ピクニック用の場所も用意されている。

Arlington Memorial Bridge was proposed by Daniel Webster and considered by Congress in 1851, approved in 1925 and completed in 1932.

Arlington Memorial Bridge (Pont Commémoratif d'Arlington); il fut réalisé par Daniel Webster, étudié par le Congrès en 1851, approuvé en 1925 et achevé en 1932.

Die Arlington-Gedächtnis-Brücke wurde von Daniel Webster entworfen, im Jahre 1851 vom Kongreß in Erwägung gezogen; 1925 akzeptiert und 1932 vollendet.

Puente Conmemorativo de Arlington: fue propuesto por Daniel Webster y tomado en consideración por el congreso en 1851; fue aprobado en 1925 y completado en 1932.

アーリントン記念橋の建設は１８５１年にダニエル・ウェブスターの提案により国会で討議されたが、１９２５年にようやく可決、１９３２年に完成した。

Tomb of the Unknowns in Arlington Cemetery. Day and night, a lone sentry paces back and forth before this tomb, whose inscription reads: "Here rests in honored glory an American Soldier, known but to God".

Das Grab des Unbekannten Soldaten am Heldenfriedhof von Arlington. Vor diesem Grab patrouilliert Tag und Nacht eine einsame Wache auf und ab; die Inschrift dort besagt folgendes: "Hier ruht in ewiger Verehrung ein amerikanischer Soldat, den Gott allein kennt."

Tombeau du Soldat Inconnu au Cimetière d'Arlington. Nuit et jour, une sentinelle monte la garde devant le tombeau, sur lequel on peut lire: "Ci-gît, honoré dans sa gloire, un Soldat Américain, connu seulement par Dieu".

Tumba del Soldado Desconocido en el Cementerio de Arlington. Dia y noche, un centinela solitario desfila de un lado al otro delante de ésta tumba, cuya inscripción dice: "Aquí descansa en digna gloria un Soldado Americano, que sólo Dios conoce".

アーリントン墓地にある無名戦士の墓。昼も夜も
この墓の前を一人の歩哨が歩調正しく歩いている。
銘刻文には「ここに神のみの知る一人のアメリカ兵士が
栄光に包まれて眠る」と記されている。

The adopted son of George Washington, George Washington Parke Custis, built the Mansion on a hill on this former Lee estate in the early 1800's. His daughter, Mary, and her husband and military commander, Robert E. Lee, lived here with their 7 children.

Le fils adoptif de George Washington, George Washington Parke Curtis, construisit la Villa qui s'élève sur cette colline, sur l'ancienne propriété Lee, au début du XIXe siècle. Sa fille, Mary, et son mari Robert E. Lee, commandant dans l'armée, vécurent ici avec leurs 7 enfants.

Anfang des 19. Jahrhunderts ließ der Pflegesohn von George Washington, George Washington Parke Custis, seine Villa auf diesem Hügel, im ehemaligen Lee-Besitztum, bauen. Hier lebten seine Tochter Mary und ihr Mann Robert E. Lee, ein Kommandant, mit ihren 7 Kindern.

El hijo adoptivo de George Washington, George Washington Parke Custis, construyó la casa sobre este cerro en la expropiedad Lee a inicios del siglo XIX. Su hija, Mary y su marido, el comandante militar Robert E. Lee, vivieron aquí con sus 7 hijos.

ジョージ・ワシントンの養子ジョージ・ワシントン・パーク・カスティスは１８００年代の初めに元リー家の所有地であったこの丘の上に大邸宅を建てた。彼の娘のメアリーとその夫で陸軍司令官のロバート・E・リーは七人の子供とともにここで暮らした。家の近くには古いアーリントン円形劇場がある。

John F. Kennedy Grave. Here burns the eternal flame which was lighted during the burial service. The Arlington Memorial Amphiteatre has a seating capacity of about 5,000 people.

La tombe de John F. Kennedy. Depuis le jour des obsèques, une flamme éternelle illumine le site. Le Arlington Memorial Amphitheater peut accueillir environ 5 000 personnes.

Das John F. Kennedy Grab. Hier brennt das ewige Licht, das während des Begräbnisses angezündet wurde. Das Arlington Memorial Amphitheater fasst etwa 5.000 Menschen.

Tumba de John F. Kennedy. Aquí se haya la llama ardiente encendida durante el funeral. El Anfiteatro Arlington Memorial tiene capacidad para 5.000 personas sentadas.

ジョン・F・ケネディの墓。埋葬式の際に灯された永遠の火が燃え続けている。アーリントン記念円形劇はおよそ5千人を収容できる。

The U.S. Marine Corps Memorial depicts one of the most dramatic events of World War II, the raising of the Stars and Stripes on Mt. Suribachi, Iwo Jima.

Le Mémorial de la Marine commémore l'un des événements les plus dramatiques de la Seconde Guerre mondiale, le hissage du drapeau américain sur le Mont Suribachi, Iwo Jima.

Das U.S. Marine Corps Memorial stellt eines der dramatischsten Ereignisse des zweiten Weltkriegs dar, das Hissen der amerikanischen Flagge auf dem Mt. Suribache, Iwo Jima.

El monumento al Cuerpo de la Marina de los Estados Unidos representa uno de los más dramáticos eventos de la Segunda Guerra Mundial: el izar la bandera sobre Mt. Suribachi, Iwo Jima.

合衆国海兵隊記念碑には第二次世界大戦でもっとも劇的な
できごとの一つが刻まれている。それは硫黄島の摺鉢山に
星条旗がひるがえる瞬間である。

Old Town Alexandria is a unique experience with shops, historic sights and a view of the Potomac River. The picture below shows famous Captain's Row; pictures on bottom, historic Gadsby's Tavern and the Boyhood Home of Robert E. Lee. Picture bottom right depicts the George Washington Masonic National Memorial.
Construction was finished in 1932.

Une myriade de boutiques, des monuments historiques et un magnifique panorama sur le fleuve Potomac vous attendent à Old Town Alexandria. La photo sur le côté représente le célèbre Captain's Row; les photos du bas représentent la Taverne de Gadsby et la maison natale de Robert E. Lee. La photo en bas à droite représente le Monument National à George Washington, dont la construction fut achevée en 1932.

Old Town Alexandria ist eine einzigartige Erfahrung mit Geschäften, historischen Sehenswürdigkeiten und der Aussicht auf den Potomac. Das Photo unten zeigt die berühmte Captain's Row; Abbildungen unten, die historische Gadsby'S Tavern und das Boyhood Home von Robert E. Lee. Das Photo unten rechts zeigt das George Washington Masonic National Memorial, dessen Bau 1932 abgeschlossen wurde.

La Old Town Alexandria es una experiencia única como negocios, lugares históricos y una vista del río Potomac. La imagen siguiente muestra el famoso Captain's Row; las imágenes en la parte inferior, la histórica taverna de Gadsby y el Boyhood Home de Robert E. Lee. La imagen inferior derecha, representa el Monumento Nacional Masonico a George Washington.
La construcción fue terminada en 1932.

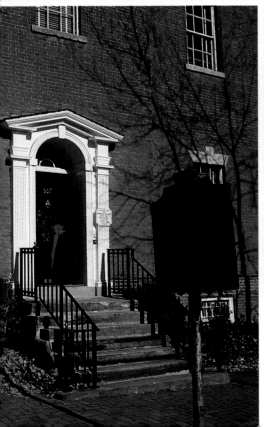

オールド・タウン・アレキサンドリアでのショッピング、
それに歴史的な景観とポトマック川の眺めは実にユニークで
楽しい経験だろう。すぐ下の写真は有名なキャプテンズ・ロー、
その下は、左が歴史的なギャツビーの旅籠、右はロバート・E・
リーが少年時代暮らした家。一番右は１９３２年に完成した
国立ジョージ・ワシントン記念塔。

Mount Vernon, the home of George Washington, is beautifully situated on the west bank of the Potomac River, 15 miles south of Washington, D.C. It was erected about 1743 by Lawrence Washington, half-brother of the First President. George Washington subsequently inherited the estate with thousands of acres of rolling land. It was the family seat until 1860, when it was purchased by the Mount Vernon Ladies Association, as a national shrine.

Mont Vernon, la demeure de George Washington, est merveilleusement située sur la rive occidentale du fleuve Potomac, à 15 miles au sud de Washington, D.C. Elle fut construite vers 1743 par Lawrence Washington, demi-frère du Premier Président. George Washington hérita, par la suite, de la propriété et de milliers d'acres de terres vallonées. Elle demeura le siège de la famille jusqu'en 1860, date à laquelle elle fut achetée par l'Association des Dames de Mont Vernon, comme Sanctuaire national.

Mount Vernon, Wohnsitz von George Washington, befindet sich in zauberhafter Lage am Westufer des Potomac-Flusses 15 Meilen südlich von Washington D.C. Er wurde um das Jahr 1743 von Lawrence Washington, dem Halbbruder des ersten Präsidenten, erbaut. In der Folge erbte ihn dann George Washington, einen Landsitz mit tausenden Morgen bewirtschafteten Landes. Er blieb bis zum Jahr 1860 Familiensitz der Washingtons, bis er dann von der Gesellschaft der Damen von Mount Vernon gekauft wurde, und heute ein Nationaldenkmal ist.

Mount Vernon, la casa de George Washington, está bellísimamente situada en la orilla oeste del Rio Potomac, a 15 millas al sur de Washington D.C. Fue erigida alrededor del 1743 por Lawrence Washington, medio hermano del Primer Presidente. George Washington heredó sucesivamente la propiedad con miles de acres de tierra ondulada. Esta fue la sede de la familia hasta 1860, cuando fue comprada por la Asociación de Damas de Mount Vernon, como una reliquia nacional.

ジョージ・ワシントンの家、マウント・ヴァーノンは
ワシントンD．C．の15マイル南、ポトマック川西岸の美しい
場所にある。1743年に初代大統領の異母兄弟ローレンス・
ワシントンによって建てられた。ジョージ・ワシントンは
その後この数千エーカーに及ぶ起伏に飛んだ土地を相続した。
1860年までは家族の屋敷として使われていたが、
マウント・ヴァーノン婦人協会が国の聖地として購入した。